FAITH MOVES MOUNTAINS

A SHORT STORY ON BHAKTI KI SHAKTI

GOPPINI KALYANI GARG

ISBN 979-888606009-6

To Lord Panduranga and his Leela .

Copyright : www.wallsnapy.com

Contents

Foreword

We all know and are aware of the western word called " Love", but in reality, we do not have the proper understanding of that word ...

Love in Sanskrit or Hindi is known as " Prema, Priti or Maitrithvaa because India is a country of unconditional Prema bhava and Sacrifice ie Tyaga.

And one of these Rasas or Bhavas is the "Bhakti Bhava" where a person surrenders himself or herself to others without any expectation ... for any sort like our mothers do.

To understand the four types of " Love" 'sahajā' (सहजा) · 'ābhyāsikī' (आभ्यासिकी) · 'viṣayajā' (वषियजा) · 'samā' (समा)please check Nityānanda Miśra youtube channel where he speaks on these Four Types of Love in an explicit way.

Today here the author Suviśrutā Kalyani GopalKrushna has shown a different angle of "Love" ie " Prema" through Kora Kumbar's story.

Let us Enjoy the story ..by having a hot cuppa of kadak chai.

Enter Caption

Preface

या कुन्देन्दुतुषारहारधवला या शुभ्रवस्त्रावृता
या वीणावरदण्डमण्डितिकरा या श्वेतपद्मासना।
या ब्रह्माच्युत शंकरप्रभृतृभिरिदेवैः सदा वन्दिता
सा मां पातु सरस्वती भगवती निःशेषजाड्यापहा

Ya Kundendu Tusharahara Dhavala Ya Shubhra Vastravrita
Ya Veena Varadanda Manditakara Ya Shveta Padmasana
Ya Brahmachyuta Shankara Prabhritibhir Devaih Sada Pujita
Sa Mam Pattu Saravatee Bhagavatee Nihshesha Jadyapaha

Salutations to Devi Saraswati, Who is pure white like Jasmine, with the coolness of Moon, brightness of Snow and shine like the garland of Pearls; and Who is covered with pure white garments, Whose hands are adorned with Veena (a stringed musical instrument) and the boon-giving staff; and Who is seated on pure white Lotus, Who is always adored by Lord Brahma, Lord Acyuta (Lord Vishnu), Lord Shankara and other Devas, O Goddess Saraswati, please protect me and remove my ignorance completely.

Enter Caption

Acknowledgements

I thank my mother for narrating Kora Kumbar's story .

I also thank notionpress.com for giving me this platform for writing this story here for the future generations to read it .

Finally I thank Goddess Saraswati for helping me narrate this story here .

ᐅᐅᐅ

Prologue

To Naam Dev questions Vittala replies " I am crying because my priyaaa bhakti is in pan and misery".

Ahhh..nnnn who is the bhakt that has made our Lord Panduranga cry like this , Naam Dev thinks aloud in front of idol ..

With no reply coming from Panduranga , Naam Dev understands the underlining message and goes in search of that priyaaaa 'Bhakt' of the Lord …

While Jumping from one Village to Another Village by singing Panduranga's bhajan ….,Naam Dev and others saints land up in Kora's Village …

Naam Dev and Other Saints creates an enthusiasm amongst the villagers and this news spread like a wild fire .

1

In a village near Pandharpur , there lived a potter named Kora .. he was a Vittal Bhagat .His profession was of making pots out of clay but because he did have any business sense or due to his bhakti on Vithoba ie Vitalla he used blindly trust people who used to say " I will come later and " but then they never come back ..to him ... and for some Kora used to give the clay for free.

This had affected his lifestyle which was well accepted by "Tulsi" his wife .She never complained about it .

Life went by for them especially for Kora Kumbar until one fateful day

2

Hari

Tulsi somehow managed to get some rice, a few lentils for them.

After cooking the food with the items borrowed from the neighbours for them, she starts to feed Hari ..their son...

Hari ... her baby was spilling the food onto the ground as he did not like the taste of the food.

Tulsi Devi understood it and...

Playfully she told her son " Beta...I know you do not like the food without tuup in it ie "Ghee" in Marathi, so I will go out and check with neighbours and will come back soon with some tuup for you until then no...going out from this place ..".

Here, we can get to see a mother's love for her child and their neighbours' friendliness...

3

Kora Kumbara 'stranscendental state.

While going out to grab some tuup for her child Hari Mrs . Kora Kumbar ie Tulsi Devi leaves the gates of their house by requesting Kora the potter to take care of their son Hari who is inside ...playing as she sees her husband hit the clay mud with his legs by singing Vitalla Vitthobha completely lost or unaware of the worldly happening...

Tulsi Devi informs him again and goes to bring some tuup for their son Hari from the neighbors.

Meanwhile...Hari comes out of his house to the lawn where ...Kora Kumbar was stamping the clay mud by singing Vital's names continuously...

Lost in the world of Vithoba, he could not hear his son Hari calling or feel his legs as it was raining heavily... He just kept on singing Pandhuranga's bhajans.....

And calling his name with his raised hands in the air while doing his work...

Hari Died Then and There

ᗽᗽᗽ

4

Kora Kumbar

ᠵᠵᠵ

Kora Kumbar 's wife Tulsi Devi on returning home starts looking for their son Hari ...., but she could not locate him.

Tulsi Devi went out and politely questioned her husband Kora about their son's Hari whereabouts.

Kora did not respond...as the question did not reach his brain to get registered ...

Suddenly her eyes swept through the clay mud on which Kora the potter was working, there she saw a tiny sweet pair of legs .. tugged to his legs and feet lying dead.

Kora.....Mr.....Potter she screams ....finally making him jump out of the transcendental state...

Looking at his dead son Hari he says " Hari was Pandurang gift to us which he has taken away with him today"

Tusi Devi ....hearing this statement got annoyed and infuriated to such an extent that...

Tulsi Devi was forced to scream by saying " I will destroy all the images, dolls of your Vithoba".

Hearing these words he runs behind with a sharp substance to hurt her.

" Stop!!!!" " "Don't Touch ME " henceforth Tulsi Devi says by giving him Lord Panduranga 's promise i.e. his 'Shapath' or 'Kasam'.

Kora....stops and accepts it, Tulsi Devi runs inside their house and cries out profusely in front of the lord and asks him " Why he did play with her like this ?", "What was her mistake?".

ᠵᠵᠵ

5

Tulsi Devi

Days, months pass by without each other making any contact..

One day ...Tulsi Devi wished for a child and she could do anything with him as she had tied him down with a promise.

Later in the evening, she thought of an idea," Why don't I get him married to my sister 'Shanti' through which I would get another child?"

Here ...what can you feel or make out of this situation ...

Please fill this blank......____

For me it is a classic example of possession kind of love

♥♥♥

Enter Caption

6
The Village Journey

Kora...I wish to make a visit to my father's village...

Okay..., no problem " When will we be leaving ?" He questions.

"Tomorrow" she responds ..

And sleeps.

Kora also sleeps beside her without touching, keeping a 1 ft distance from her.

The next day they go to Tulsi Devi's father's village...

On their arrival and after exchanging formal greetings with one another ...

Tulsi Devi takes her father inside and asks him " What do you think of Shanti and Kora Kumbar 's marriage?".

What ?...

Have you gone mad ? he asks.

Then thinking about their poverty and Shanti's security he agrees....

Kora, are you ' Okay ' with my other daughter Shanti ... getting married to you ? he asks with a question mark look on his face...

"Yes, father" Kora Kumbar replies, touching his father's feet.

ᗐᗐᗐ

Enter Caption

7
Marriage and Home Coming of 'Shanti'

The father gets them married, but while sending them back to their village, Shanti's father says "Treat my daughter 'Shanti' like Tulsi Devi Koraa…".

"Yes Sure father !" he says and takes his leave beginning with his way back journey way.

They reach home … after a long tiresome journey, Now Tulsi instructs her young sister 'Shanti'to do Pati Seva for Kora so that she can get benefits/ fruits of their bond …

Shanti…. Goes to their room with water and milk, only to be instructed by Kora not to come close. Now on your lord is "Panduranga" and not me….. In a state of shock, she follows his instructions and goes off to sleep …

The next day morning, Tulsi questioned "Shanti" about her 'Pati Seva' experience.

Shanti narrated the entire sequence of events of the night.

"Datt…Panduranga !!!! what I have done ….and why this kind of suffering has to befall on my sister now" Hey Viitalla she questioned through her silent tears …

Life went for them, Now Kora Kumbar'brother's wife taunted them a lot ..initially, she used to give /lend food or money for Tulsi to look after her family by making note of it in a dairy expecting Tulsi would pay her back …. But now an addition into the family made Kora Kumbar's brother's wife humiliate them in open by telling their loan amount with interest openly …

They kept quiet ….ie Tulsi and Shanti.

They went inside their beautiful house quietly, Kora did not change a bit and was continued praising his Lord Vittala ....with every breath...
Now tell me/us can this happen in this century?

Wife/ girl would easily leave the husband/boy if he did not cater to her needs / meet the requirements of their house.

ᗡᗡᗡ

8

Ranga Coming

Finally one day, Kora Kumbar's sister-in-law (his older brother's wife)decided to sell Kora's house as he did not repay the loan taken by his Wives 'Tulsi Devi' and 'Shanti'.

She informed the head of the village who seemed to agree with her. Kora too accepted the decision happily because of his love for Vithoba...

Auction Happened!

The house was sold!

When....Kora along with his wives Tulsi and Shanti were about to leave their house, Ranga held his hand and said: " Where are you going Pitaj this is your house now I bought it for you ".

Kora the potter would not understand and comprehend, he said: " I do not have any son now and the son which I got from my lord Panduranga got snatched away from me after the unfortunate fatal accident ..".

Oh ho, Pitaaji !! Ranga says with a smile plastered on his lips.

"Pitaaji, I am that potter boy who sits a few shops away from your place and whenever I used to see you...I used to think of you as my Pitaajii since we do not have family Rukumini added as Ranga was sparking and looking into their eyes".

Rukmini is correct "Baba," he says and keeps their luggage back inside the attic of their house.

Finally, Kora accepts as his son ... and starts leading his life by singing Vithoba's name while making earthenware pots.

ppp

Enter Caption

9

Tulsi and Shanti

One day while Kora was working with his clay mud and working on his potter machine

Tulsi and Shanti his wives decide to hold his hand despite the प्रतिज्ञा(pledge) of not touching them which Kora Kumbar had taken a few months ago before his another marriage with Shanti, Tulsi's younger sister (Potter was bound by a शपथः Shapathah i.e promise. A promise which we take in front of God by taking water in our hands, involving the panch bhuttas we take a promise/ शपथः Shapathah/ प्रतिज्ञा PLEDGE for something regardless of its importance but we do not dare to break प्रतिज्ञा or promise which we have taken in front of God and nature)

So.... later that night, Shanti and Tulsi hold his arms and hands while he was fast asleep... from both sides.

The next day, when he gets up and sees his hands-on Tulsi and Shanti's body. Kora Kumbar panics and says "Panduranga Panduranga !!!!! how did happen?, I have done an unforgivable offense i.e. mistake, for such a mistake on my part, I should not these two hands " and runs towards the potter machine and chops off his arms.

With a regretful feeling, Tulsi and Shanti were forced to do everything for him.

❦❦❦

Enter Caption

10

Naam Dev and Other Saints

One day Tulsi sitting idly thinks over the past events and cries in front of Panduranga, "Why you give a lot of sufferings to us alone, Kora my husband does your bhakti a lot despite my several tantrums towards him and his bhakti ".

Naam Dev and other saints while singing Panduranga bhajans in Pandharpur In front of the idol ..see a difference on their ishta Vithoba's face

.

Naam Dev and Other Saints question Vithoba " Hey Panduraya.... The one who makes us cry...., why is he i.e you crying today like this ?".

To Naam Dev's questions, Vittala replies " I am crying because my priyaaa bhakt is in pain and misery".

Ahhh..nnnn who is the bhakt that has made our Lord Panduranga cry like this, Naam Dev thinks aloud in front of the idol...

With no reply coming from Panduranga, Naam Dev understands the underlining message and goes in search of that priyaaaa 'Bhakt' of the Lord ...

While Jumping from one Village to Another by singing Panduranga's bhajan ...., Naam Dev and others saints land up in Kora's Village ...

Naam Dev and Other Saint create enthusiasm amongst the villagers and this news spread like a wildfire.

ᑭᑭᑭ

Enter Caption

11

Panduranga's Gift

When Kora comes to know about the arrival of great saints of his ishta , he jumps in joy and runs towards the ground where they have assembled by clapping his hands .

The people who saw this sight ...informed Tulsi Devi.

A shocked Tulsi Devi ...

Immediately Replied !!!

"I cannot believe it, please take there"

Tulsi Devi says with tears filling her eyes ...

She then requested them to take her to the place where Bhajan Mandali had assembled singing Vitthoba's bhajans.

Seeing her Kora Kumbar dancing and clapping his hands enjoying the bhajans sung by Naam Dev, Tulsi Devi wished and asked Panduranga "If you can give my husband's hands back then.... Why cannot you bring back my child Hari !!!!! to me".

Immediately... as if he was waiting for her to ask

Tulsi Devi heard a voice calling "Aai Aai" means Mother in Marathi in the crowd.

Tulsi Devi looked everywhere and in the direction of the voice, Lo Ho she saw Hari her dead son in the same way and in the same structure walking towards her.

Hugging him ..

Tulsi Dev went to her house shouting "Ranga Ranga look who has come !!!!"

ꕥꕥꕥ

, but there was no reply from their house, and the doors of the house were open too. She went inside in search of Ranga ..., but she could not find him anywhere.

12

Epilogue

A few moments later, Ranga and Rukmini appeared in front of them, blessed Kora, Tulsi, Hari, and Shanti...

Tears rolled down their cheeks...

With Gratitude in their eyes, they prostrated before them...

Then Rukmini asked Kora Kumbar to stop making promises or taking pledges like he took before and lead a happily married life with his two wives and 'Hari'.

The End

❥❥❥

13

Bonus Poem on Love

Anusuya Attri's Love

Anusuya is a character in mythology who was a great 'Pati Varta' that even the tri murtis Devis could not tolerate her and in order to test her chaisty they sent their husbands whispering a plan into their ears with a clause of being naked.

Initially, the husbands did not like it but later accepted it as the tri mutri Devis were sitting over their heads with a hammer.

Future what happens to the TRI DEVAS we will see through this poem...
One Day ,
Narad comes to Satya Loka ,
With iron channa ,
Filled in Glass ,
Giving it to Saraswati Devi ,
He asks her to cook for him
She Tries but fails ,
Then......,
Naradji goes and comes to ,
Vaikunta ,
Meets MahaLakshmi there ,
With Iron Channa in his hand,
Filled in a glass ,
He asks her to cook for him,
She too fails in achieving her task.

Then he goes and comes ,
To Mount Kailash,
Meets Paravati there ,
With Iron Channa in his hand,
Filled in a glass,
He asks her to cook for him,
Parvati also fails in her task ,
He goes by saying " I will get it done in Goloka"
Who in Go loka has the capacity to do ,
They Enquire with pride,
You will see it soon Naradji tells them by singing his mantra,
'Narayan Narayan'.
Coming down to Goloka he goes to Attris Ashram,
Meeting Anusya Devi ,
He says ,
Mother will you cook ,
This Iron Channa in his hand,
Filled in a glass for me ,
Yes Son ,
Please have sit ,
Looking at the iron channa ,
She sets her cooking utensils on her fire ,
Keeping iron channa filled glass in the vessel ,
Closing it with a lid ,
She thinks of her husband only ,
The Iron Channa gets cooked ,
Adding Spicies to it ,
Son here to take it ,
She says ,
Handing it over to Narad Muni Ji ,
Dhanyawad Mother Anasuya Devi !!!,
Naradji says with a smile and leaves Attri's ashram.
Entering the Satya, Vaikunta and Mt Kailash Again ,
Having a a a naughty smile ,
The Tri Mutri Devi question ,
What happened Narad ,
He show the cooked iron channa,
Then.....,

Saraswati,
Lakshmi ,
Parvati's head fall in shame ,
And ,
They feel insulted,
Narad " How can the Goloka Vasi" Be more powerful than us,
Because is great 'Pati Vrata' ,
Narad Tells ,
And leaves the three lokas for doing 'sanchar',
To accuse and spoil her name,
They conspire,
Before they could do something ,
Brahma ,Vishnu, Mahesh warm them ,
Off the power to destroy them,
The Tri Mutri Devi's did not heed their advice,
They went forth with the plan,
They had conspired ,
Whispering their plan with a clause
' Anasuya feeding/ giving you all beeksha by being naked',
The Tri Devi were shocked ,
They tried to protest ,
But....,
Everything went waste ,
As the Tri Mutri Devi got adamant ,
To teach Rishi Patni a lesson.
The Tri Dev reached goloka,
Went to Attri's ashram as 'Brahmins' asking for 'Beeksha',
With a clause ,
Anasuya Devi invited them inside ,
Devi we want beeksha from you ,
Its has a .... clause ,
That you will give us beeksha ... ,
'By being naked' in front us ,
Without much thinking she nodes as ,
She could see who these people were ,
With Divine Vision.
Anasuya Devi went inside to seek advice from her husband,
On this matter ,

Attri's strange reply "Do it as per their wish ",
Forced her to think ,
By taking the water in hands with which she did Paduka pooja of husband,
Hail all the panch bhuttas ,
" If I am true Pati Vrata please help me in fulfilling the wishes off these brahmins",
She sprinkles water on them,
Making them into 6month old baby,
Anasuya Devi feed them rice and milk,
Nakedly...
Putting them into 3 different cradles to sleep,
Later on,
Chaos happened in Satya loka, Vaikunta and Mt Kailasa
As heads we not there,
After a lot of searches,
30thousand Devi and Devatas questioned Tri Mutri Devis about their heads,
On their persistent queer,
They replied,
To test Anasuya Dev's 'Pati Vrata',
They sent them down to 'Go loka'
Immediately everybody went to Attri's ashram,
Was welcomed Anasuya Devi,
The Tri Mutri Devis did not wish to take anything from her,
They only wanted to see their husbands.
Saraswati Devi ....,
Lakshmi ,
And Paravati questioned her about their husbands,
Oh, they,
Are
Sleeping there,
Anasuya replies with a smile,
Feeling ashamed,
They ask her to bring them back,
"In their original form",
Smiling she does,
Hail all the panch bhuttas,

" If I am true Pati Vrata please help me in fulfilling the wishes of these brahmins",
She sprinkles water on them,
The Tri Dev come back to their original form,
With a promise of coming as her children...,
Anasuya Devi begets three babies,
Brahma as 'Chandra ',
Vishnu as 'Dattatrya '
And,
Mahesh as 'Durvasa'...

ppp

Thank you ..for reading this story.

♡♡♡